Jeter
Hero in Pinstripes

Sports Publishing Inc.
www.SportsPublishingInc.com
www.dailynewsbooks.com

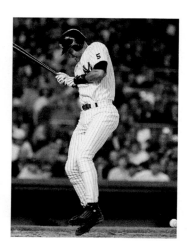

Coordinating editor: Claudia Mitroi
Supervising editor: Joseph J. Bannon, Jr.
Production director: Susan M. McKinney
Cover design: Scot Muncaster, Terry Neutz Hayden
Interior design and layout: Terry Neutz Hayden
Copy editor/Proofreader: David Hamburg
Photo editor: Eric Meskauskas and Angela Troisi
Photo production: Christina Cary

ISBN: 1-58261-359-1

Printed in the United States

www.SportsPublishingInc.com
www.dailynewsbooks.com

ACKNOWLEDGMENTS

From the moment he first signed his Yankee contract to his latest great play, Derek Jeter has remained true to the famous words of Yankee legend Joe DiMaggio: "I want to thank the Good Lord for making me a Yankee." The writers and photographers of New York's famed *Daily News* have richly chronicled Jeter's meteoric rise through the minor leagues to superstardom with the Yankees.

Bringing Jeter's memorable moments to life every day in the *Daily News* takes the hard work and dedication of many people at the paper. When we first approached the *Daily News* about this project, we received the overwhelming support of Les Goodstein (Executive Vice President/Associate Publisher) and Ed Fay (Vice President/Director of Editorial Administration). Among others at the paper who were instrumental in assisting us in this project were John Polizano, Lenore Schlossberg, Eric Meskauskas, Angela Troisi, Mike Lipack, Vincent Panzarino and Faigi Rosenthal and her great staff. From the *Daily News* sports department, we specifically want to acknowledge the cooperation and support of editor Leon Carter.

Space limitations preclude us from thanking each writer and photographer whose work appears in this book. However, wherever available, we have preserved the writers' bylines and the photographers' credits to ensure proper attribution for their work.

And finally, I am grateful for all the support and hard work of those at Sports Publishing Inc. who worked tirelessly on this project: Joe Bannon Jr., Terry N. Hayden, Susan McKinney, Christina Cary, Victoria J. Marini and David Hamburg.

Claudia Mitroi
Coordinating Editor

CONTENTS

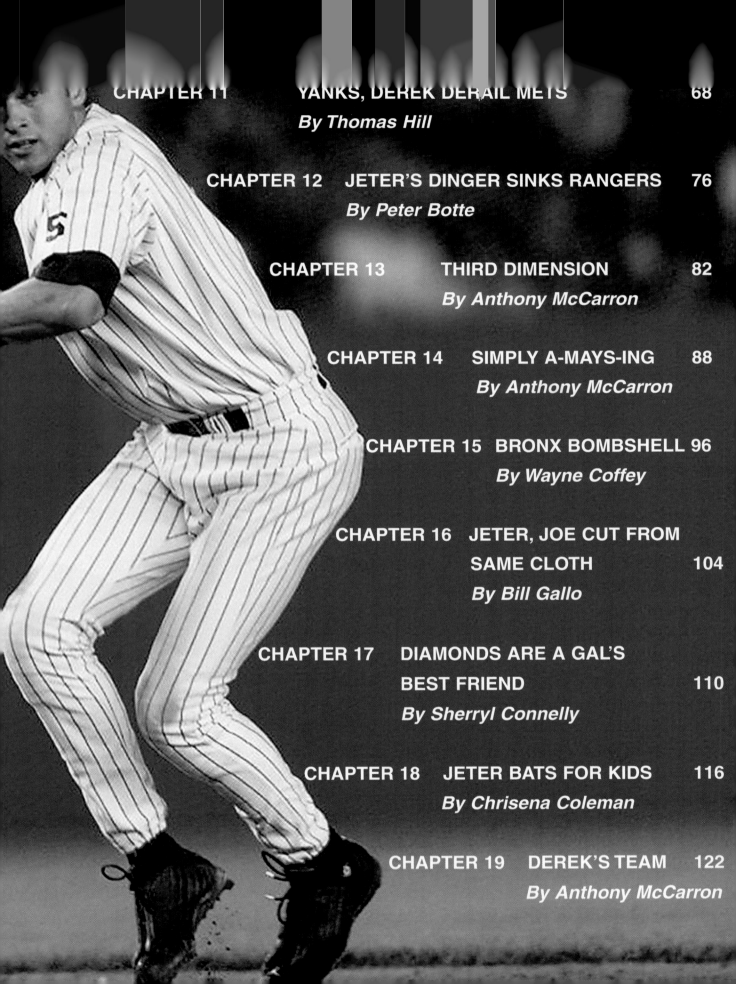

Jeter

CHAPTER 1

Derek Jeter was signed as the
first-round draft pick to a contract

700 G LANDS YANKS' FIRST PICK

worth more than $700,000.

BY JEFF BRADLEY

6/29/92

Jeter

The Yankees' previous signing of a rookie sensation, Brien Taylor—who signed for $1.55 million—resulted in long, drawn-out negotiations that dragged on for a long time. With Jeter the signing seemed relatively painless.

"I'd call it a direct antithesis," said Jeter's agent Steve Caruso, "to the negotiations with Brien. We disagreed over a few things, but it was all handled very professionally."

Jeter, a 6-3, 175-pound shortstop out of Kalamazoo (Mich.) Central High School, will report to the Yankees' minor league complex in Tampa tomorrow to begin play for the Yankees' Rookie League affiliate in the Gulf Coast League.

He is considered a "true" shortstop by the Yankees' minor league staff.

"He is a five-tool player," said Bill Livesey, the Yankees' director of scouting. "He can hit, hit with power, field, run and throw."

Jeter, the sixth pick overall and first high school player selected in the draft, hit .508 this past spring for Kalamazoo Central. He had signed a national letter of intent to attend the University of Michigan on a baseball scholarship, but opted instead to begin his pro career.

"There's no doubt that I'll go to college at some point," said Jeter, who had a 3.8 high school grade point average. "The money [the Yankees paid] was definitely a plus, but their interest was what made the difference. I got the feeling they were very high on me."

Yankee Sage

CHAPTER 2

"My dream was to play for the Yankees, to play for them in the World Series.

FORGET AGE— JETER'S TRUE YANKEE SAGE

Now to get all that in one year, it's kind of hard to talk about."

BY IAN O'CONNOR
10/20/96

Just when you figured Derek Jeter would not slip, would not once appear lost in New York, he parked his car on Second Avenue. The city finally got to him. Early on a Friday morning, either a tow-truck or a thief made off with his leased Mercury. Jeter lost the car, some clothes, a few CDs. He could not understand. He was parked alongside a meter, legal and everything.

"If anybody finds it," he said at his locker, "just give me the pants and you can have the car." Rookie mistake, Jeter was told. "Guess so," he said.

Jeter had a few coming to him. Tonight, the first rookie shortstop to start for the Yankees in 34 years is scheduled to start the World Series, if the rain doesn't wash away another game. To punctuate an unlikely year of grace, he has hit .415 in the postseason, handling his position without effort, accepting his burden without pause.

At 22, Jeter acts like the oldest man on the team. He outplayed one of his idols, Cal Ripken Jr., in the five-game defeat of Baltimore. The other day, he declared he wouldn't surrender an inch to Atlanta's indomitable pitchers.

His teammates take him at his word. Three of the heavy-mileage veterans, Mariano Duncan, Charlie Hayes and Darryl Strawberry, all said they haven't seen anything like him. Jeter, they swear, was born to play the position. Truth is, the kid decided he wanted to be the shortstop for the Yankees when he was 10 years old.

"I can't put it into words," Jeter said. "My dream was to play baseball for the Yankees, to play for them in the World Series. Now to get all that in one year, it's kind of hard to talk about."

So the veterans talk for him. They say rookies in the past have shown them skill or poise, but not both. Jeter is big and quick, sure and smooth. He hit .314 and drove in 78 runs during the regular season, hit .350 after the All-Star break.

When the lights got hotter, Jeter got better. The pressure of New York, of a pennant race, wasn't a deterrent, but a source of positive juice.

"The thing that sets Derek apart from everybody else," said Hayes, "is that he's not afraid to fail."

Regular Season
.314

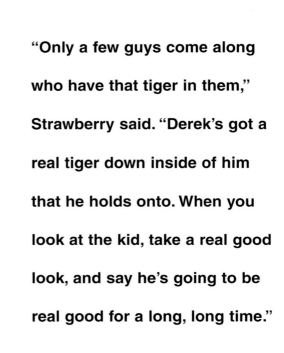

"Only a few guys come along who have that tiger in them," Strawberry said. "Derek's got a real tiger down inside of him that he holds onto. When you look at the kid, take a real good look, and say he's going to be real good for a long, long time."

This was hardly a gradual process for Jeter. Joe Torre was banking on the rookie to play shortstop from April to October.

Torre wasn't risking his job at the time; George Steinbrenner's advisers wanted Jeter in place. But all involved were hoping for a reliable glove and a .250 batting average.

What they got instead was baseball's version of a natural-born killer.

"As soon as I saw Jeter in spring training, I said to myself, 'I don't even know how one guy can have so much ability,'" said Duncan. "I knew right away he had a chance to be a superstar. The way he handles himself is something you don't see in rookies.

"He plays like he belongs in the major leagues. Every time he's in a pressure situation, he comes through. I like him so much because even after a bad game he comes to the park with the right attitude. It's like he's been playing in the majors for five years."

"Everyone in the media said I was a rookie who couldn't handle the playoffs," Jeter said. "Sometimes you get hits and sometimes you don't. If I go 0-for-the-World Series, I'm still going to tell you I wanted to be out there."

The Yankees want him out there, for Jeter inspires faith. He said he wants the ball hit to him in the last inning of the last game, with the whole World Series at stake.

"I'm not afraid to make mistakes," Jeter said. "As long as I learn from them."

Derek Jeter is a fast learner, on the fields of the Bronx, on the streets of Manhattan.

"Next time," he said, "I won't be parking on Second Avenue."

Dreams

Come
True

CHAPTER 3

They came out of the dugout, first
Derek Jeter and then
Bernie Williams, and the two of
them ran right across the words

WILLIAMS, JETER FIND DREAMS COME TRUE

"World Series" that had been
painted so brightly on the grass of
Yankee Stadium.

BY MIKE LUPICA
10/20/96

Jeter and Williams are the most gifted of all the young Yankees. But watching them take the field, the last time they would take it before the Series, was like watching them run right into the oldest dream there is in sports: Wearing this uniform. Playing in this place. Being a Yankee in the World Series.

Before the kids dreamed of being Michael Jordan, they dreamed all that. Jeter knows.
When he was a child, his grandmother used to bring him with her from New Milford, N.J., to watch the Yankees play on summer weekends. They would sit in the bleachers and Derek Jeter would watch Don Mattingly at first and Willie Randolph at second and Dave Winfield, his favorite, in the outfield.

He would look out to shortstop and see himself. "I have a better view where I am now," Jeter says.

Once it was Joe DiMaggio running out to center field and Phil Rizzuto running with DiMaggio, veering off and going to shortstop. In the World Series of 1941, the first they played together, the first of so many they played together, DiMaggio was 27 and Rizzuto had just turned 24. It was the last time the Yankees had such young talent at the two most glamorous positions on the field.

Until now.

Yankee stars of this October, they play their first World Series together. Watching them take the field at Yankee Stadium, take the stage this way, it is impossible to believe it will be their last.

Derek Jeter was born in Pequannock, N.J., and his family lived in New Milford. Then he did most of his growing up in Kalamazoo, Mich. But there were always visits to his grandmother. There were those handful of precious visits to Yankee Stadium. Someday he would make it out of the bleachers.

Someday he would be in the World Series with the Yankees.

When he runs out to his position for Game 1, when he stops at short while Bernie Williams keeps going to the outfield, it will be the first time Derek Jeter has ever attended a Series game in person.

"This is what you've always thought about," Jeter said. "From the time you start playing ball, you think about the World Series. And if you've ever been inside Yankee Stadium, you think about playing here."

"I'm not sure people understand how good the two of them can be," Joe Girardi says.

Girardi, one of the best guys in the clubhouse, one with the best seat in the house to watch both Jeter and Williams play every day, shakes his head, not just talking about the center fielder, but the shortstop as well.

It is a few minutes before 1:00, two days before Game 1 of the World Series. Williams is supposed to be out on the field. He grabs his glove and runs up the runway behind the Yankee dugout and up the steps and onto the famous baseball grass. Jeter is just a bit ahead of him.

Bernie Williams smiles. The smile says: So this is the way the World Series is supposed to look. Young players, old Yankee dreams. Not some movie field of dreams. The real one.

It's
Unanima

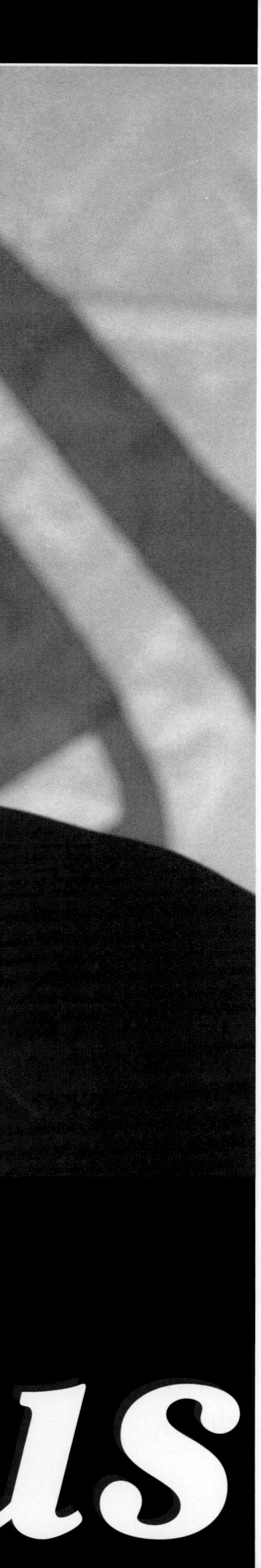

It began with a fifth-inning solo homer off Dennis Martinez, followed by a spectacular

IT'S UNANIMOUS: JETER GETS ALL VOTES FOR AL ROOKIE OF THE YEAR

over-the-head, run-saving grab of Omar Vizquel's blooper into shallow left-center field.

BY BILL MADDEN

11/5/96

From that attention-grabbing afternoon, on a blustery, snow-delayed Opening Day in Cleveland, Derek Jeter embarked on his personal journey to star status as the Yankees' shortstop.

It was a dream he began cultivating as a kid, and yesterday it culminated in his winning the

AL Rookie of the Year by a unanimous vote.

"I wanted to make the team, play well and win a world championship," Jeter said last night at Yankee Stadium. "To do all three and win this award, too . . . well, I'm still dreaming."

Suffice to say Jeter dispelled all the doubts, starting on day one of the Yankees' championship '96 season when he served notice as a shortstop to be reckoned with.

"I know a lot of people doubted me," Jeter said. "For me, though, I had a lot of confidence in my ability. I felt that if I just did what I had done in the minor leagues, I'd be successful."

"I think that play he made on Opening Day—a play that only Ozzie Smith makes with regularity—opened some eyes, as did the homer," Torre agreed.

Jeter's 78 RBIs were the most by a Yankee shortstop since Frank Crosetti's 78 in 1936. Torre even conceded it is possible that Jeter could evolve into a Cal Ripken-type of high-RBI man.

"You don't hit .300 with 600 at-bats unless you've adjusted to all the adjustments other people have made on you," Torre said.

"I need to get stronger," Jeter said, "but I got a long way to go before I get too strong."

"This isn't going to go to my head," Jeter vowed, glancing over at his father. "I can't go home if my head is too big. My parents wouldn't let me in the house."

Grand
Slam

CHAPTER 5

Derek Jeter continues to be the
most productive Yankee

JETER'S GRAND SLAM!

when it comes to off-the-field
business deals.

BY RICHARD WILNER

6/25/97

The popular Yankee shortstop has hit an endorsement grand slam, signing four major deals, including two national contracts for roughly $1.5 million a year, since helping lead the Bronx Bombers to the World Championship last year.

Fila Holding SpA, the footwear and apparel company, the largest of the deals, a reported $1 million a year, will have Jeter in Fila spikes and wristbands for four years.

Jeter has emerged as one of the best-liked major leaguers and one of the most popular among corporations looking for clean-as-a-whistle athletes to push their products.

The Fila deal follows a national deal Jeter and his agent, Casey Close of Cleveland-based IMG, inked with Pepsi. The Pepsi deal is reportedly valued at $250,000 annually.

any deal but also the national exposure and
the style of the campaign," said Close.

Jeter wants to agree with the tone of any long-term
marketing strategy and to be able to finance his
Turn 2 Foundation charity, Close added.

Seal It

CHAPTER 6

It was only one more hand to shake,
one more face to forget, until the
man opened his mouth and froze
Jeter like a two-foot curve.

DEREK AND PARTNER
CAN SEAL IT

"Derek, I'm Peyton Manning. You're
having some career."

BY IAN O'CONNOR
2/10/98

Derek Jeter was heading for the Garden door Sunday night, signing more autographs than Kobe Bryant, when yet another basketball fan approached to talk baseball. It was only one more hand to shake, one more face to forget, until the man opened his mouth and froze Jeter like a two-foot curve.

"Derek, I'm Peyton Manning. You're having some career."

The shortstop quickly lateraled the compliment, and the two began speaking the exclusive language of the young and gifted. Behind them, out of the conversation, a third athlete was saying that Jeter was a lucky soul. Not because Jeter had made the acquaintance of a star quarterback, but because he was about to make the acquaintance of a star receiver.

"Joe Montana," Alex Rodriguez said, "just found his Jerry Rice."

On a night to watch basketball players and meet football players, Jeter was wondering about baseball players. He was sitting next to his friend and enemy, the great Alex Rodriguez of Seattle, at the NBA All-Star Game, asking him for a scouting report on a second baseman Rodriguez had worked with during some exhibition games in Japan.

CHAPTER 7

"De-Rek! De-Reeeeeeek!"
the girls scream, their arms

TO GAL FANS, NO ONE'S NEATER THAN JETER

outstretched with autograph pads
covered in colored spangles.
"I love you De-Rek!"

BY TARA GEORGE
9/13/98

High-pitched squeals ripple through Yankee Stadium as hyperventilating girls leap to their feet and screech.

The ball game suddenly seems like a Leonardo DiCaprio appearance. And that can only mean one thing: Derek Jeter is on the field.

To most Yankee fans, the 24-year-old shortstop is one of the heroes of the best Yankee team in recent memory.

But to hordes of young girls, Jeter is the "sweet," "cute" pinstriped star of their intense teenage fantasies.

"They send him piles of fan mail—letters, autograph requests and pictures of themselves surrounded with Jeter memorabilia," a Yankee spokesman says.

His correspondence arrives at the rate of about 20 pieces a day—far outstripping the other players—and amasses in buckets at his locker, awaiting his personal reply.

The girls know his sports statistics, but they'd rather discuss his other assets, such as his "sweet face," "nice eyes" and "really, really cute butt."

"I've been here 42 years and I've never seen girls go fanatical about a ballplayer like this," says Kenneth Spinner, a Stadium vendor. "Every time his name is announced, they go berserk."

James Mitchell, an usher, confirms the madness.

"They go nuts. He's sexy . . . the girls love him . . . from 16-year-olds to about 40," he says.

The young Jeterettes live him, breathe him and run websites devoted to him. They paint his number—2—on their faces, plaster their walls with his image and craft posters to hoist at games in the hopes they'll appear on the jumbo screen and Jeter will notice.

"Oh my God! Oh my God! We were really, really close," an excited Stefanie Dicrocce, 13, of Long Island tells her family as she rushes back from the autograph pack above the dugout, her face flushed and sweating.

"It was, like, the highlight of my life."

arbitration process always is a gamble. Sometimes it's
...ust about the case and the facts," said Yankee general
manager Brian Cashman.

...as Close argued Monday, Jeter, who finished third in the AL MVP
...is worth more to the Yankees than numbers.

...ek means so much more to the New York Yankees than
...s runs scored (127), batting average (.324) and other
...stics," Close said. "He has every intangible quality—a

"The lesson is arbitration is not like the judicial system. Those men who are making the decision are swept away by a lot of things," Steinbrenner said. "This is the first time I can remember—and it's perfectly proper—where the popularity of a player played a great part."

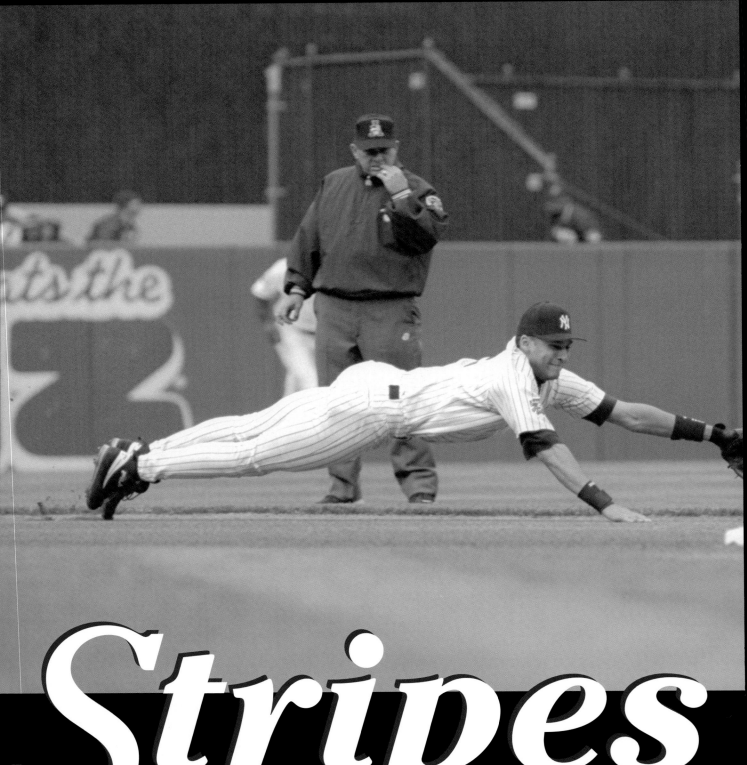

Stripes
Forev

3-Run Dinger

Pitchers across baseball have been unable to adjust to Derek Jeter all season, but the

JETER'S 3-RUN DINGER SINKS TEXAS

Stadium's famed bleacher creatures have altered their roll call to accommodate the Yankees' all-everything shortstop.

BY PETER BOTTE

6/16/99

When it came time to chant Jeter's name
the rabid right-field fans yelled,

"MVP! MVP!"

"What am I going to do, turn around after 50 games?" Jeter asked afterward.

Jeter did not acknowledge the fans for nearly one minute. But the bleacher creatures are clearly on to something.

Jeter's three-run homer was the exclamation point on a six-run outburst in the second inning to support David Cone's latest winning effort. The Yankees' tidy 6-2 victory over the Rangers took less than 2 ½ hours to complete before 28,200 at the Stadium.

"He's just phenomenal," Cone said. "He gets big hits, home runs. He's the key to our lineup."

"He's virtually carried us the first third of the season."

The offensive numbers he continues to post are staggering. Jeter has been on base in all but one of the Yankees' 62 games on his way to a remarkable .380 batting average, trailing only Tony Fernandez's .403 mark in the American League.

His team-high totals in home runs (12), RBIs (46) and walks (39) project to 31, 120 and 102 over 162 games.

Jeter's home run just missed landing in the very section where the early-game chant summed up exactly what type of player the people of New York believe Jeter has evolved into.

"That's what I thought they were saying," Joe Torre said of the MVP chant. "But I just knew he wasn't going to turn around."

Third
Dimen

CHAPTER 13

Jeter knew there would be intense
interest in the lineup switch
that dropped him from his

JETER ADDS THIRD DIMENSION

customary second to the third
spot in the batting order.
It could be a permanent move.

BY ANTHONY McCARRON

6/20/99

Jorge Posada looked across the Yankees' clubhouse at his pal Derek Jeter.

"That guy,"

Posada said, "I don't talk to him anymore. He hits third one time and then he doesn't call, he won't talk to you."

Of course, Posada was joking. He and Luis Sojo razzed Jeter a little before Friday's game when Jeter batted third for the first time in his major league career, but nobody else in pinstripes said much about it to the shortstop.

"People say it's a big responsibility," Jeter said. "But I say playing shortstop is a big responsibility, too."

Would hitting third, generally considered the spot reserved for a team's best hitter, change how Jeter is perceived in baseball? "That's up to you guys with the pens," he said. When someone mentioned that Mark McGwire also bats third, Jeter said, "Don't start comparing me to Mark McGwire."

More likely, Jeter has to worry about being mentioned in the same sentence with Babe Ruth, another famous No. 3 batter in the Yankees' lineup.

"Everyone probably wants to hit third," he said. "It's a situation where you're going to be in a lot of RBI situations. I don't think you ever go in and say, 'I'm hitting second today, I can take it easier.' You still want to have good at-bats, still want to put the ball in play, get your hits.

"I'm only hitting third in the first inning and the only difference is my first at-bat comes about a minute and a half later.

"You don't change your approach any."

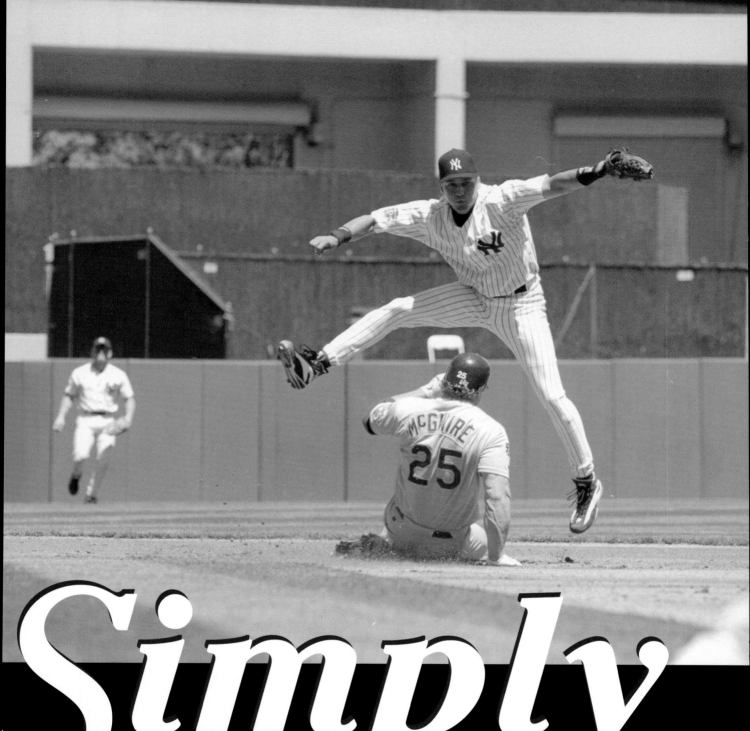

Simply
A-mays-i

CHAPTER 14

Call it the infielder's version of
the famous catch Willie Mays
made in the

YANKEES AGREE
JETER CATCH IS
SIMPLY A-MAYS-ING

1954 World Series
and link the names Randy Velarde
and Vic Wertz for trivia fodder.

BY ANTHONY McCARRON

6/21/99

Derek Jeter,

with his back to home plate, ran flat-out for

ankee shortstop Derek Jeter—surprise—made an amazing play in yesterday's 4-2 loss to the
ngels. If you missed the highlights, here's a synopsis so you're ready for some watercooler
banter this morning.

With Anaheim's Darin Erstad at second and one out in the third,
Randy Velarde lofted a pop that seemed destined to land between
Jeter, center fielder Bernie Williams and left fielder Chad Curtis.
Jeter turned around and, with his back to home plate, ran flat-out for
the ball and made an over-the-
shoulder catch that David Cone
likened to that of an NFL wide
receiver.

he ball and made an over-the-shoulder catch.

Then, à la Mays once more, Jeter whirled around and threw to Chuck Knoblauch, doubling up Erstad, who was already rounding third.

"I don't remember a better play by a shortstop, going out that far," Joe Torre said. **"He went out to the left-field position, damn near."**

"I managed Ozzie Smith and he used to practice that play every day. Jeter covers more ground than Ozzie did."

"I thought it was in nowhere's land," Jeter said. "I just ran to the ball and didn't hear anyone [calling for it]."

Mays made an over-the-shoulder grab against Wertz in what has become one of the most rerun baseball highlights ever. He made a great throw after the catch to prevent a run from scoring.

Jeter's play ended the inning and Cone said it was a huge moment at that juncture of the game.

When Jeter was told of Cone's comparison to a wide receiver, he grinned and said, "I never played football. I was too skinny. I guess that's as close as I'll come."

Chili Davis, dressing in a nearby locker, needled Jeter, saying, "You'd be the kind of receiver I would have loved to see coming across the middle in high school. Imagine what this game would be missing if you played high school football against me."

The door swings open and out steps the New York Yankees' All-World, All-Heartthrob shortstop, looking as dashing in a dark pinstriped suit as he does in the white pinstriped suit he wears in the Bronx.

It is an off-night for the Yankees, so Jeter is hosting the annual benefit auction for his charitable foundation, Turn 2. By the time the night's bidding is done, he has raised nearly $210,000 for charity. It is but one more spectacular number in a season that has been crammed with them for Derek Sanderson Jeter, the kid from Kalamazoo, who, at 25 years of age, seems to redefine the city's standard for stardom with each passing week.

Don Zimmer, the Yankees' 68-year-old bench coach, has spent half a century in professional baseball. He is asked about Jeter's 1999 work in progress.

"I can't remember any middle infielder doing what he's done, offensively and defensively, over these three months," Zimmer says. "He's just very, very special."

The notion of Jeter getting better is indeed almost unimaginable. So is the idea that he could handle things any better. In only his fourth season, Jeter has not merely emerged as one of the best players in the game. He has evolved into a long-legged revelation, a turn-of-the-millennium icon who, unlike so many of his superstar contemporaries, has no bloated ego, no whacked-out sense of entitlement, no attitude. With Jeter, the words "Yankee class" are much more than a tired organizational mantra. They are true.

How well-mannered and humble is Derek Jeter? He calls his manager Mr. Torre. He calls his bench coach Mr. Zimmer. He opens—and does all he can to answer—all his own mail. When asked about comparisons to New York sports heroes such as Joe Namath, Walt Frazier and Reggie Jackson, he is quick to rein it in. "That's unfair to them," Jeter says. "I mean, I've played three full years. It's flattering, but you've got to play longer than that to be mentioned with those guys."

"He cares about people," Jorge Posada says. "He does everything the right way. It's tough not to like him."

Spend any time around Jeter, and you can't help being struck by yet another endearing quality: his gratitude for where he is. He is playing out a childhood fantasy, starring for the team he grew up rooting for. He is a pinstriped poster boy for the young, handsome and richly blessed.

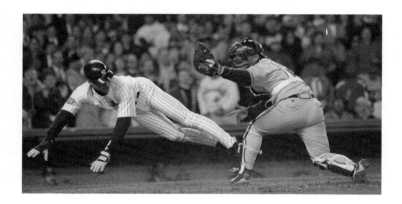

Three and a half years and two World Series rings into his career, he is on a fast track to Monument Park—and takes none of it for granted. It is no idle gesture when Jeter gallops happily down the blue and white tunnel from the clubhouse to the Yankee dugout and jumps up to touch the little sign that hangs overhead and quotes Joe DiMaggio ("I want to thank the Good Lord for making me a Yankee").

Says Jeter, "I wouldn't trade what I'm doing for anything. I'm living a dream."

Dr. Charles Jeter, Derek's father, is a former drug and alcohol counselor who now runs his son's foundation. "People look at him now and think it was always easy, but I'm here to tell you it wasn't. Even in the spring training before his rookie year, he played terrible down there." Charles Jeter says he is proud of the way his son

worked his way through it, with a confidence as strong as his arm from deep in the hole.

Posada still marvels at how Jeter—the rookie—set the emotional tone for the Yanks' comeback from two games down in the 1996 Series, leading off Game 3 in Atlanta with a double. "He just kept swinging, and we followed him," Posada says.

One of Jeter's favorite TV commercials is the Nike spot in which Michael Jordan talks about how many times he has failed over the years.

"You're going to make mistakes," Jeter says. "I don't care who you are. You can't be afraid. A lot of people, when they are doing well, walk around with a smile on their face. I think you can tell a lot about a person with how they react when things aren't going well."

Says Zimmer, "Some guys come in here and have a look on their faces like they've just come out of jail. Like it's a job. The thing with Jeter is that it's still a game. He has fun. He laughs. He says funny things to the manager. He's a kid playing baseball." Probably no other Yankee could've pulled off the tension-lifting stunt Jeter did last year before Game 4 with the Indians in Cleveland, the Yanks' dream season perilously close to ruination. In the dugout, Jeter walked up to Torre, poked a finger in his chest and said, "Mr. Torre, this is one of the biggest games you've ever managed in." Jeter has reprised the routine many times since. Torre enjoys it.

Before every game for four years, Jeter has walked up to Zimmer, taken off the coach's hat and rubbed his bald head. Then he rubs Zimmer's round belly. When Zimmer's nubs of hair get a bit long, Jeter will come over to him and say, "Tighten it up."

The flip side of Jeter's pressure-free approach is a passion for perfection that is second to none. He lives in Tampa in the off-season so he can have easy access to the Yankees' complex. He spent countless hours there last winter, lifting weights, retooling his swing, learning to turn on the ball better. The payoff? He's on a nearly 30-home run pace, leads the league in triples (7) and leads the Yanks in RBIs (55). A year ago, the buzz was that as fine a player as Jeter was—and he was third in AL MVP voting—he was not in the offensive class of Rodriguez and Garciaparra, two of the premier power-hitting shortstops in history. Nobody is saying that this year. Certainly not Tiger lefty Justin Thompson, who watched Jeter lay his black 32-ounce Louisville Slugger on a shin-high fastball and drive it over the left-center-field wall at the Stadium last week.

The combination of Jeter's glorious skill, sunny spirit and uncommon maturity explains why he has become the unofficial Yankee captain.

"He's the youngest [starter], but he's the oldest in so many ways," Posada says.

It was not as if nobody expected big things from Derek Jeter when he first put on his pinstripes. Uniform No. 2 is not given to anybody by accident. But who could've foreseen that he'd just keep getting better, that he'd wear his stardom with such grace, that he'd grow into the sleek standard for Yankee shortstops right before our eyes?

"I'm not surprised," Tino Martinez says. "I'm just surprised it's happened in four years." It's a great life, and doesn't Derek Jeter know it? As he runs off for pregame stretching and touches the Joe DiMaggio sign one more time en route, Jeter smiles.

"If you're looking for complaints,"
he says, "you're talking to the wrong guy."

As he sifted through a stack of fan mail, Jeter was asked a simple question:
Who would you want to be if you could be another athlete for a day?
"Michael Jordan," Jeter said, without hesitation.

"I mean, this guy can't go anywhere," Jeter said. "You could put him in any country on Earth. To be at the top like he was, I'd just like to see what it would be like for a day, maybe a week. After that it might get to be too much."

Jeter's admiration for Jordan is not hard to detect. Attached to his locker wall is a silhouetted photocopy of a Jordan dunk. On the floor of the locker are a dozen pairs of baseball cleats with the same silhouette.

It is the logo of Brand Jordan, a newly launched Nike subsidiary that hired Jeter as one of its charter endorsers.

Jeter first met Jordan in the fall of 1994, at an Arizona instructional camp during Jordan's fling with baseball.

"He was very nice, very down-to-earth," Jeter said. "I was very impressed with the way he treated me."

Same
Cloth

It goes without saying that with free agency, there will be little chance in the future

JETER, JOE CUT FROM SAME CLOTH

to see very many stars stay attached to their original team.

BY BILL GALLO

8/8/99

Playing baseball with one club for an entire career is something as old-fashioned as the fedora hat. When you realize that Cal Ripken Jr. has spent the last 19 years playing for one club—the Baltimore Orioles—you have to figure he's straight out of those olden days, when fans could jot down their favorite team's lineup without checking the box score.

There are ballplayers who just do not look right in any uniform except the one they were meant for. Take Joe DiMaggio—can you see him in anything but pinstripes?

There's a current Yankee whom I feel the same could be said about. This would be Derek Jeter, who is rapidly making us all believe that he is the greatest Yankee shortstop of all time. Jeter is a pinstriper, and—free agency or no free agency—it looks like he'll be wearing that classy uniform for the rest of his baseball career.

In this day and age of spoiled superstars, Jeter is one who knows how to handle the sudden fame he's achieving very well. This is a young man who comes from good stock, and I got a hint of this by talking to his mother, Dot Jeter.

It was during Mother's Day when I talked to this charming lady from Kalamazoo, Mich. Our conversation took place in 1997, and then she proudly gave her age as 43 and said she was the mother of two children, a 22-year-old son and a daughter, 17. Dot told me that her husband Charles, a substance-abuse therapist and Ph.D., were the proud parents of Sharlee and Derek.

Sharlee was then a high school senior about ready to enter Spelman University for girls in Atlanta. **Derek,** of course, is the well-mannered shortstop for the Yankees.

Growing up, Jeter always had this dream of one day becoming a Yankee.

I remember asking Dot Jeter if she thought her boy would ever achieve his dream.

"I told him what my husband told him:

If that's what you want, **Derek,** then you must work hard.

There are **no** shortcuts."

Realizing what a close-knit family
this was, I asked her to characterize
Derek's relationship with his dad.
"It's always been close. My husband
would [and still does] call Derek 'the
ol' man,' a term of endearment. Like I
said, we're a close, lovable family."

So, there you have a little picture of the star
Yankee shortstop. What you see in him through
his family is a strong steadiness, and he carries
this on and off the field.

Here's a guy whose Yankee uniform
suits him to a tee.

And you can almost bet he'll be wearing it
for a long time.

Baseball
Diamon

Bats For Kids

CHAPTER 18

To 15-year-old Leticia Thomas,
Derek Jeter is more
than a superstar ballplayer.

JETER BATS FOR KIDS TRYING TO GET AHEAD

She considers the Yankees
shortstop a friend and
a role model.

BY CHRISENA COLEMAN

10/22/99

Derek has been there for Leticia, picking her to become one of
Jeter's Leaders, a member of Derek's educational program
that helps inner-city kids who do well in school.

And she'll be there for him tomorrow, jumping up and down in
front of the television every time Jeter goes to bat during the
World Series opener against the Atlanta Braves.

The Bronx teen is one of 20 students in the group, which
promotes healthy living, academic achievement,
physical fitness and community service.

CHAPTER 19

Call it a head check.
It was early in the 1997 season,
and Joe Torre was thinking about
his young shortstop, Derek Jeter.

FLASHY JETER IS OUT OF THIS WORLD; THESE YANKEES ARE DEREK'S TEAM

Jeter was coming off the type of
rookie season normally concocted
in a fuzzy movie devoted to the
idea of baseball as myth.

BY ANTHONY McCARRON
3/28/00

Jeter was the reigning AL Rookie of the Year, the Yankees the reigning champs, and the city was in love with both. The biggest city's biggest game hasn't stung its biggest player. And if New York is at the center of the baseball universe again, then Jeter is both ambassador and prince.

Jeter is moving closer to Yankee legend status and already is a player who transcends the game—people who know or care nothing about baseball are aware of Derek Jeter.

"Culturally, he appeals to such a wide range of people," teammate David Cone said. "Everywhere you go, there are Derek Jeter fans. He makes us into sort of a traveling show in every town we go to."

Before last season's World Series, Jeter was making about $1 million

a year in endorsements, in addition to his $5 million Yankee salary.

This year, Jeter will make $10 million from the Yankees.

The two have been negotiating a long-term deal (believed to be seven years

for $118.5 million) that would make Jeter among the highest paid in baseball.

Plugging Jeter's name into an Internet search engine can reveal more than 15,000 sites devoted to all things Derek.

It is a moment from a meaningless spring training game. A wobbly line drive off the end of someone's bat knuckled just past Jeter's glove, reaching left field. A base hit. Even though he missed the ball, Jeter smiled. It was not rueful, he was not chiding himself. It was, according to Torre, a smile that showed how much fun Jeter was having.

"He just enjoys himself," Torre said. "You don't find that as much anymore with all the pressure and stress in the game. And he even realizes he's more than a ballplayer now, that people are interested in more about you than just